SECRET AGENTS OF THE WILDERNESS

VOLUME 1
Guardians
OF THE Trails

TOP SECRET AGENTS REVEALED!

RON GUILEY

Guardians of the Trails

VOLUME 1 TOP SECRET AGENTS REVEALED

Text and Most Photos by Ron Guiley

Copyright © 2020 by Ron Guiley

All rights reserved. This book or any portion thereof may not be reproduced or used in any manner whatsoever without the express permission of the publisher except for the use of brief quotations in a book review.

Printed in the United States of America

First Printing, 2020

ISBN 978-1-7326125-3-2

Deschutes Publishing LLC

P.O. Box 1877
Bend, OR 97709-1877

RonGuileyAuthor.com

Dedicated to Taya, Isaac, and Gracie.

Photo by Christina Jen Photography, Bend, OR

EDITED BY

Jessica Page Morrell

Many thanks for your editing, instructional expertise, advice, and articles.

SPECIAL THANKS

Lavinia Davidson of **Bow Wow Salon**, Bend, Oregon, for your wonderful work keeping the Guardians looking good on the trails. Even Crazy Lil.

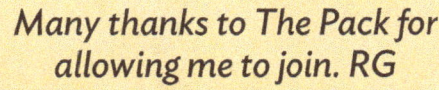

Many thanks to The Pack for allowing me to join. RG

This amazing collection of secret missions includes:

11

The Secret of Magic Dust

Humans are anxious to know how Crazy Lil can talk to animals. Do her special powers really come from rolling in Mother Nature's Magic Dust?

49

Watery Graves at Dillon Falls

When flying birds suddenly plunge into the river and don't come up, the dog park is buzzing with rumors of evil spirits. Can the Guardians save the day?

FROM THE CANINE NEWS NETWORK

This SPECIAL ANNOUNCEMENT

TOP-SECRET UNIT EXPOSED!

CRAZY LIL REVEALS SECRET OF MAGIC DUST

The recent release of government secrets has uncovered a Special Operations Team known as **Guardians of the Trails**.

Their mission is to make the trails safe for dogs, humans and other animals.

The Guardians have become heroes, and much of it is because of the *special powers* demonstrated by the smallest member of the force, Lily. Also known as Crazy Lil, she has used her magical abilities many times, allowing her to speak to animals in their own languages. These rumors have the humans excitedly panting.

Is Crazy Lil right? Do her special powers really come from rolling in Mother Nature's Magic Dust or is Bella right and she's simply rolling in ordinary dirt?

What do you think?
TODAY, CRAZY LIL WILL SHOW US ALL HOW SHE DOES IT.

Members of the Guardians

Bella is a red standard poodle who was a nerd while still a puppy and grew to be super smart. She is Peaches' mother.

Lily (also known as Crazy Lil) talks with Mother Nature and rolls around in Magic Dust to gain mysterious powers. She's a miniature poodle.

Peaches is a young, apricot standard poodle. She's super smart like her mom, runs and jumps like a deer, and always has a smile on her face.

Dad is the old, slow human the Guardians allow to tag along on their adventures. He carries the water and always brings special treats. Like bacon.

Top-Secret Unit Exposed

The Guardian's base of operations is hidden in a small town in Central Oregon. This means they're only a short run to the snowcapped Cascade Mountains, the dense blanket of ponderosa pine forests that cover the rolling eastern foothills, and the Deschutes River with its rough, wild waterfalls. This is the wilderness territory they patrol as agents for Mother Nature. It's a dirty, hazardous job, but someone has to do it.

The Secret of Magic Dust

Good day ladies, gentlemen, and reporters. I'm Bella and beside me is Peaches. We're two of the Guardians of the Trails. Today, for the first time, the US Forest Service has agreed to inform the public about our team's secret work in the mountains and wilderness areas of Central Oregon. Now I'll introduce the third member of the team, Lily.

Thanks, Bella, and welcome.
We're delighted to have you learn
all about our covert missions.

By the way, Dad calls me, "Crazy Lil"
because he thinks I'm crazy rad.

I was chosen by Mother Nature to receive unusual powers from her Magic Dust by using her top-secret method. These powers allow me to talk to other animals in their own languages. This means we can find lost animals or learn about possible dangers.

Flashback! (WE'RE GOING BACK IN TIME...)

How and why did Lily receive special powers from Mother Nature? We're glad you asked.

When Lily was just a tiny, wiggly puppy, she was the kindest pup in the litter. Instead of shoving smaller puppies away from their shared food, she would help them eat. When she grew into a bigger, adventurous youngster, she would protect smaller puppies from the bigger bullies.

But one warm spring morning something amazing took place in the dark forest. A curious ground squirrel was watching the puppies' rough and tumble wrestling in a grassy meadow. Suddenly a lean, mean coyote leapt out and gazed hungrily at the squirrel, who was trapped against a rock. The coyote wore a wicked smile as he stalked closer, licking his chops.

Lily leaped to the rescue, chomping with all her might on the coyote's hind leg and thrashing her head from side to side. The coyote yelped and leapt away, shocked and startled that a poodle with small, sharp teeth had attacked him from the rear. But then he stopped and turned, his cruel, yellow eyes glaring down at the puppy and saw... a Lily-Burger.

"Run!" Lily shouted at the squirrel. There was a lump in her throat and she swallowed hard as she watched him disappear. The snarling coyote could gulp her down in a few bites, but she wasn't giving up without a ferocious fight. She spun around to face the cold eyes and drooling jaws, but was amazed to see the terrifying coyote had vanished. The sky was suddenly filled with a bright, shimmering rainbow and a cheery female voice spoke to her.

"Lily, I'm Mother Nature, and I'm so proud of you. I've watched you from the day you were born. When you were still a puppy you were already strong and kind. And now you've risked your own life to save a helpless squirrel. Because of your gentle heart and brave spirit I have an important mission for you that means you'll receive unusual powers. Draw on them to protect my wild places and creatures. You can use these powers any time you need them by rolling in my Magic Dust."

So Lily gained her powers and the Guardians were born, fulfilling the missions given them by Mother Nature herself.

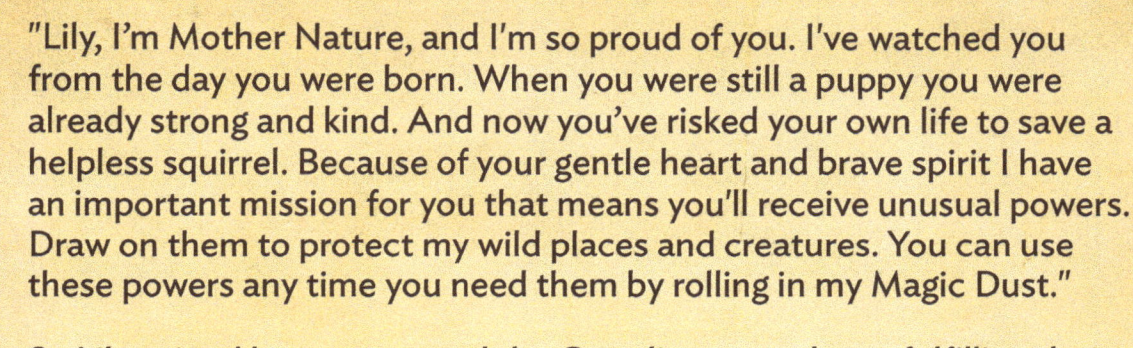

And now, back to our adventure...

The Guardians often learn about a lost or dangerous animal from other dogs, but sometimes these reports are hard to track down. Sometimes we search the river's steep, bushy banks...

...and snoop in hiding places for dangerous creatures...

...but today we still can't find the threat. To solve this mystery we first need to locate it. What can we do?

Seriously! What a mystery!

There are only three canines who can wear the Guardians of the Trails Badge, and Peaches is one of them. Let's hear what she says.

There's only one thing we can do, Lily. Use the Magic Dust. **Dude!** There's a huge bird with a long, sharp beak perched high on that old snag.

Good eyes, Peaches. It's a great blue heron.

Woodsy Wisdom from the Guardians

Great blue herons are common water birds found in Central Oregon. They are the largest of the herons found in North America and stand about 4 feet tall. Herons have keen eyesight and long, sharp beaks to eat fish and other water creatures. They will stand motionless for long minutes until an unlucky fish or frog wanders too close. They fish near marshes, rivers, and oceans, and will even land at a fish pond in someone's back yard and gobble down a quick snack of goldfish. And I don't mean the cracker kind.

Well, Lily, what about the Magic Dust?

I just sent a message to Mother Nature. She'll answer me soon.

Whoa! How Could Bella Join the Guardians When She Doesn't Believe in Magic Dust??

It all started when she was just a puppy......

Bella gazed sadly at her puppy brothers and sisters as the humans swung open the gate to the great outdoors and the litter barreled through the doorway, laughing wildly as they raced out into the sunlight. All except Bella.

The other puppies made fun of her. They said she was lazy. But Bella wasn't lazy. She was a nerd.

The humans had constructed a high, strong enclosure for the rowdy litter and covered the floor with pages from their college textbooks. New, clean pages were spread out in the pen every day, and while the other puppies laughed and played outside, Bella stayed indoors and read all the pages. After eight weeks the humans had used up all the pages from their old books, and Bella had become one of the smartest poodles of all times. But the other puppies still laughed at her.

"You never come out and play. You're no fun." And it hurt Bella's feelings terribly.

"What good is it to be a mental giant if no one likes me?" And tears filled her eyes.

That is, until one day a roly-poly, white miniature poodle named Lily came to find her. The chubby, curly-haired puppy walked up to Bella and grinned.

"I'm a Secret Agent of the Wilderness with special powers from rolling in Mother Nature's Magic Dust. She says you're the smartest dog around and could help me keep the wilderness safe for dogs, humans, and other creatures. You'd be doing a great service to the environment."

Bella frowned and shook her head, her long, soft ears shaking side to side.

"Secret agent? I never heard of you." Lily nodded her muzzle with a twinkle in her eye.

"Well, if you'd heard about me I wouldn't be a secret agent, would I?"

Bella had to admit that made sense. Her studies had never mentioned Magic Dust and she was sure it didn't exist, but she realized her brilliant mind now had an important purpose. And so she joined Lily and the Guardians of the Trails was born.

Now back to our adventure...

Still no sign. Ohhh, this mud feels good on my paws and the water is so cool and tasty... Now I know where the Magic Dust is located. Move out, Guardians!

Nope. It's not out here either. My nose tells me it's dead ahead.

For the first time in canine history, the Guardians of the Trails are going to let you in on the secret method.

Just like there's a right and wrong way to catch a ball, there's a right way and a wrong way to apply Magic Dust. Doing it the right way is fun and exciting.

I start the rollover slowly and then finish with a kick that will... flip me on my back and...

Presto! I'm now covered with a beautiful layer of Magic Dust! But there's still one important step: The Finish.

YES! Quick as I can, I snap up to my feet and shake to spread the Magic Dust evenly over my body. Now I possess awesome powers.

Once our assignment is completed I take a fast dip in the river and I'm all clean and back to my normal self again.

We hope you've enjoyed this peek behind the scenes. Now that our missions are no longer TOP SECRET you will be able to read about our many adventures and follow along.

OH YEAH! And now Dad gives us...**BACON!**

Now that you're in on her secret method, join us for **Watery Graves at Dillon Falls** and see how Crazy Lil solves a baffling mystery.

Watery Graves at Dillon Falls

Dillon Falls is located on the Deschutes River ten and one-half miles upstream from Bend in Central Oregon.

Swollen with snowmelt from the nearby Mount Bachelor, Broken Top and South Sister, what looks like a calm section of the river turns a blind corner. Then it drops 65 feet, starting with a fifteen-foot drop leading to Class V whitewater rapids through a steep, deep, narrow canyon. Class V are treacherous, dangerous rapids that require experience and skill to navigate.

Hello there! I'm Bella, one of the three members of the Guardians of the Trails. It's always wonderful to meet brave humans who will travel along with us on a hair-raising, dangerous adventure...

Today's spooky assignment finds us struggling to figure out why birds are disappearing into the river at Dillon Falls. The dog parks are buzzing with rumors that a strange, evil curse is at work. And now many of our fellow canines are now so afraid to visit the trail they're shaking in their collars. Bruno the Pug witnessed the birds crash into the water, so first we listened to his tale.

It was horrible! Those poor birds must have been under a powerful, evil spell to suddenly disappear like that. One minute they flew through the air and the next they crashed into the water, and we never saw them again. We raced to the bottom of the falls but there was no trace of them. They just vanished into thin air!

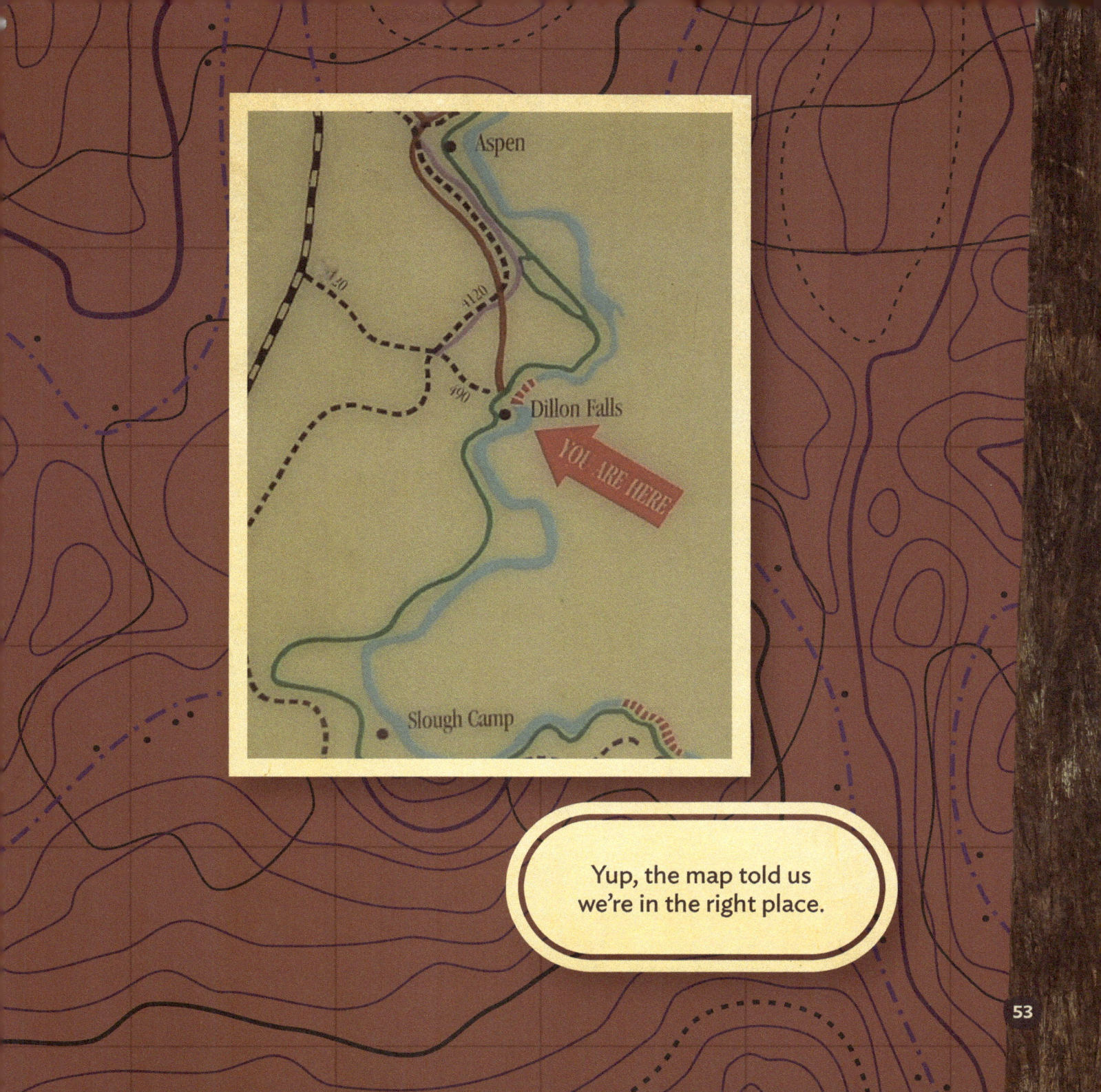

It really makes you look pretty. You should keep it.

Her sense of humor worries me. Maybe I didn't spend enough time with her when she was just a puppy...

It also worries me that we've hit a dead end. We can't find any trace of the birds. Maybe Lily had more luck.

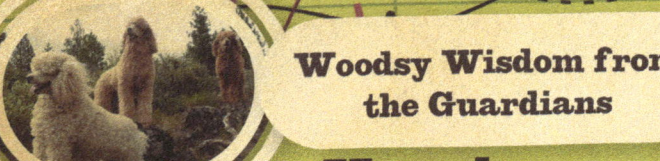

Woodsy Wisdom from the Guardians

How do you move a river and create a waterfall at the same time?

Dillon Falls was formed about 7000 y[ears] ago when a massive lava flow from La[va] Butte crept like a slow-moving beast dow[n] the forested slope toward the Deschutes River six miles away. The Deschutes River proved no match for the red-hot wall of rough, chunky lava as it covered the old river channel with a hundred feet of steaming rock. Then, like a lumbering, unstoppable bulldozer, the flow continued plowing across the river and deeper into the forest, shoving the river ahead until the lava finally cooled and halted. The river quickly began slicing a new channel, complete with waterfall, along the edge of the flow. Today, the river marks the path where lava moved a river.

A great blue heron rests atop the wall of lava that forms the east bank of the Deschutes River.

If any birds went over these dangerous falls they wouldn't stand a chance.

Woodsy Wisdom from the Guardians

How do you move a river and create a waterfall at the same time?

Dillon Falls was formed about 7000 years ago when a massive lava flow from Lava Butte crept like a slow-moving beast down the forested slope toward the Deschutes River six miles away. The Deschutes River proved no match for the red-hot wall of rough, chunky lava as it covered the old river channel with a hundred feet of steaming rock. Then, like a lumbering, unstoppable bulldozer, the flow continued plowing across the river and deeper into the forest, shoving the river ahead until the lava finally cooled and halted. The river quickly began slicing a new channel, complete with waterfall, along the edge of the flow. Today, the river marks the path where lava moved a river.

A great blue heron rests atop the wall of lava that forms the east bank of the Deschutes River.

There's no sign of any birds in the rapids all the way down the steep canyon. Now what?

There's only one thing left to do. I must call on Mother Nature and the Magic Dust, even if it's *frozen* Magic Dust. Once I roll in it and get my amazing powers, we can solve this mystery.

Oh, *YES!* That is *SO* good! And now I feel the powers flowing through me. We'll find the answer near a steamy waterfall, past a boulder path, and down a snowy stairway.

Lily, I'll always love and believe in you, even if my mom thinks you're nutty.

Up and...oomph! Hey, wait for me...

Finally. It's the steamy waterfall. How mysterious...

Full alert! Mother Nature is all around us now and she's sending an awesome bird to give us answers.

I see it, Bella, standing in the water right over there!

I see it too. And now it all makes sense.

Woodsy Wisdom from the Guardians

This is an American dipper, also called a water ouzel, named for its up and down bobbing motions. They're the only songbirds in North America that can fly in the air and also under fast-moving water. Much of their lives are spent under water, diving up to 20 feet to move rocks on the riverbed, searching for insects, fish eggs and even small fish to eat. Their diet is similar to a trout, and improving streams has helped slow the bird's declining population. Dippers can travel long distances underwater, even against the current. Bruno probably left the riverbank before the birds resurfaced.

Mission accomplished! Again! The Guardians can now spread the word that the trail's safe and there's nothing to fear. It was really those totally awesome birds, not a treacherous curse.

Dude! Guardians **ROCK!** If we had capes, we could fly....

One frigid, cloudless morning the dogs and I trudged through four inches of new snow to Big Eddy on the Deschutes River. A series of Class III rapids, it's a popular destination during summer for rafters and kayakers. But that day the newly-risen sun warmed no one on the frozen banks but me and two shaggy poodles deliriously romping in the soft white powder. Their antics subdued as we climbed down the icy lava rocks to the soft roar and stood a foot away from the churning, aqua torrent raging past. It was an experience that begged to be shared with photographs.

Thus **Guardians of the Trails, Secret Agents of the Wilderness** was born. The poodle pack, now numbering three, eagerly investigates the trails of Central Oregon and shares the adventures in photographic tales to fascinate young readers and tap deeply into that ancient, wild heritage that resides restlessly inside each of us.

But who authors the adventures? If this is truly an author's page I need to include the pups. It's true I'm the photographer and I put the stories together for publication, but it's the dogs that truly determine the story. When we hike in the wilderness or along a seldom-travelled path beside a wild river, the pack is free to follow its canine nature. As such, the poodles are as much the authors of our episodes as I. They'll go anywhere, anytime and in any weather. They never complain and always let me know they had a wonderful time. Of course, bacon helps.